BACK *to* BACK

Exploring life, death and everything

Pete Townsend

Kevin Mayhew

First published in 2001 by
KEVIN MAYHEW LTD
Buxhall
Stowmarket
Suffolk IP14 3BW

9 8 7 6 5 4 3 2 1 0

ISBN 1 84003 715 6
Catalogue No 1500418

Cover design by Jonathan Stroulger
Edited and typeset by Elisabeth Bates
Printed and bound in Great Britain

Contents

Acknowledgements

One of the issues missing from this book is *Patience*. My excuse is that I know very little about the subject. Having said that, I am eternally grateful to those people who've demonstrated this elusive ability time and time again.

Here, in no particular order of virtue, are some of those people who qualify for the cocoa-tin lid medal for outstanding patience:

Liz: 'Ain't it finished yet?'

Ed and Jane: 'Never mind, have another glass of wine.'

Billy and Sharon: 'One day, mate, one day.'

Nig and Carol: 'A curry would be nice.'

Ruth: 'Is there any chocolate left?'

Anyway, as in all good acknowledgements, thank you to the thingammys, wotsits and hoojimaflops for blah, blah, blah. And, as always, Ruth . . . I love you.

Introduction

It's quite simple, really; this book has a look at some issues that we all face from time to time. Each issue is looked at from a slightly different perspective, then there are a couple of questions to reflect on, a couple of things to consider, a brief look at what the Bible says on the subject, followed by a prayer or meditation.

You may not agree with many of my comments; in fact, they may really irritate you. Good! That's exactly why I've written them in the first place. All too often we drift from day to day: get up, stand up, clean up and eat up (not in any particular order of preference). We're faced with issues that cry out for attention, but we try to ignore them in the hope that they'll go away or that somebody else will deal with them. Wrong, big time!

Don't let the issues take hold of you, you must take hold of the issues. How you deal with them is up to you and what part you think God has to play in your life. Whatever you do, don't shut yourself in the wardrobe and hang out with all the other lifeless forms; take issue with the issues.

I hope you enjoy this book. Even more, I hope that this book encourages you to explore life and what God has to do with it all. Please feel free to let me know what you think at the email address below. And, whatever they say, it's OK to dunk custard creams in your coffee! Cheers,

Pete

Email: townie@postmaster.co.uk

The human condition _____

Life is a strange concoction . . .

During those few short minutes, when your eyes were open and your brain ticking, you couldn't help being really impressed with some of those facts that permeated your skull concerning life on earth.

Many books have been written, films produced, TV programmes created and articles conceived, about those creatures that have an amazing ability to be incredibly creative and extraordinarily destructive at the same time: the human being.

We are a fantastic creation. Read some of the facts:

- A human has 60,000 miles of blood vessels in their body.
- There are approximately 625 sweat glands in every 2.5 square centimetres of skin.
- When you blink, you use over 200 muscles.
- Babies are born with 300 bones, which reduces to 206 by the time we reach adulthood.
- A foetus acquires fingerprints at the age of three months.
- Every time you frown you use 43 muscles yet only 17 to smile!
- On average, the human body contains enough iron to make a 7.5-centimetre nail, enough sulphur to kill all the fleas on an average sized dog, enough carbon to make 900 pencils, potassium to fire a toy cannon, fat to make 7 bars of soap, phosphorous to make 2,200 match heads and enough water to fill a 50 litre tank.
- The largest human organ is the skin, with a surface area of approximately 8 square metres.
- The human body has over 600 muscles.

- The body's longest organ is the small intestine at an average of 7 metres.
- There are 45 miles of nerves in the skin of an average person.
- 300 million cells die in the human body every minute.
- The average person loses about 600,000 particles of skin every hour, almost a kilo each year (multiply that by the average life-span!).
- On average, we drink approximately 80,000 litres of water in a lifetime.
- A sneeze can travel at speeds of 100 miles per hour.
- Banging your head against a brick wall uses 150 calories an hour (although the length of time spent actually banging your head depends on who you work for!).
- The strongest muscle in the human body is . . . the tongue.
- On average, you sweat enough fluid each day to fill six Coca-cola cans.
- We breathe about 23,000 times a day.
- Most people blink about 25,000 times a day.
- The human body has fewer muscles than a caterpillar.
- When you blush, the lining of your stomach blushes too.
- Every step you walk requires the use of 54 muscles.
- There are over 100 million light-sensitive cells in the retina (think eyeball!)
- The average person falls to sleep in seven minutes.
- The thumb is the same length as the nose.
- Your foot is the same length as the distance between your wrist and elbow.
- Your eyes never grow, but your nose and ears never stop!

- When you sneeze, all bodily functions stop, even your heart.
- A third of our life is spent sleeping.
- And, finally, are you one of the 85 per cent of the population that can curl their tongue?

Life, a pretty amazing thing!

Death – it could be you!

Death, a word that nobody likes to mention in polite conversation, particularly while chewing a triple cheese-burger with extra fries. Still, as they say, it's something you can't argue with.

Characters	Bill and Bob are two exhausted old cronies. They're tired and are now finding it difficult to find the energy to smile. They've no regrets about life, well, not many . . .
Scene	The two cronies are seated on an old bench. They are surrounded by darkness and the only light is from a rusting lamp-post, next to the bench.
Props	A bench or two chairs side by side. A lamp-post which can be depicted by placing a table lamp on top of a tube or suspended from a convenient place. The two cronies are dressed simply in pale trousers and T-shirts (preferably white).
Bill	That was quite an amazing experience. *(Rubs hands together)*
Bob	*(Nods)* Mmm. Yeah, sure was.
Bill	Bit hairy at times, though. *(Looks at Bob)*

Bob	*(Thinks. Raises eyebrows and rubs chin)* Well, let me see. Yeah, I suppose you could say there were one or two dodgy moments.
	(Both characters are quiet for a few seconds. They look thoughtful.)
Bob	*(Begins to giggle)* I've . . . just . . . remembered.
Bill	*(Smiles and nudges Bob)* What?
Bob	*(Continues to giggle)*
Bill	*(Starts to chuckle)* Go on, what?
Bob	*(Wipes eyes with hand)* It was so funny.
Bill	*(Nudges Bob again)* What, what was so funny?
Bob	*(Coughs and sits upright)* Nothing.
Bill	*(Amazed voice)* Nothing?
Bob	Well, not a lot.
Bill	But enough to make you giggle.
Bob	*(Big smile)* It was really funny.
Bill	Are you going to tell me or not?
Bob	*(Tries hard not to laugh. Pats face with hands)* You really want to know?
Bill	*(Folds arms across chest. Stern face)* I wouldn't waste my time asking if I wasn't bothered.
Bob	Well . . . *(Places hand across mouth as more giggles erupt)*
Bill	*(Sighs angrily)* Oh, for goodness' sake.

Bob	*(Wipes eyes, coughs and sits upright)* I'm sorry. I really don't know what came over me.
Bill	*(Strokes chin and remains silent)*
Bob	*(Nudges Bill)* Hey, are you all right?
Bill	*(Sniffs)* Just thinking.
Bob	*(Nudges Bill again)* Tell.
Bill	*(Sighs)* OK, if you insist.
Bob	I do, I do, I do.
Bill	I was just wondering . . .
Bob	*(Leans towards Bill)* Yeah?
Bill	*(Scratches side of head)* Wondering if . . .
Bob	Yeah, go on.
Bill	*(Turns to Bob and places fist under his chin)* Whether you'd like a knuckle sandwich?
Bob	*(Sits back quickly, brushing Bill's fist away)* Get out of it, you daft mollusc.
Bill	So, are you going to tell me what caused your giggling tackle to go into overdrive?
Bob	*(Pats Bill's arm)* OK, if it'll make you feel better. Although once I've told you, you may wish you'd never asked.
Bill	Let me be the judge of that.
Bob	So be it. Right. Do you remember Daphne Widget?
Bill	Would that be the Daphne Micklethrollop who married Wally Widget?

Bob	That's the one. Well, she once told me that she saw you and Angela Stickleback in a romantic embrace a few years back.
Bill	*(Huge smile on face. Folds arms)* What of it?
Bob	Well, you know that Daphne and Angela were good friends.
Bill	*(Starts to fidget)* Yeah.
Bob	*(Tries to suppress a giggle)* It appears you left her with a souvenir of your romantic inclinations.
Bill	*(Continues to fidget and shows embarrassment)* Did nothing of the sort.
Bob	I think you did.
Bill	I really don't know what you may be referring to.
Bob	No?
Bill	Definitely not!
Bob	Are you sure?
Bill	As sure as I'm going to give you a kick on the shins.
Bob	*(Moves legs quickly out of the way)* No need to get shirty. Anyway, Angela became quite attached to the little memento of your fling.
Bill	Fling? Nothing of the sort. Couldn't perform a fling if I tried. Only put my back out if I did.
Bob	*(Rubs own back)* Oooh, just the thought of it brings tears to my eyes.

Bill	Which is just what I'll do if you don't finish telling me what you're going on about.
Bob	OK. In a nutshell. You, Angela, embrace, kisses, etc., memento of your affection.
Bill	And?
Bob	Glass jar, label, shelf, public display.
Bill	What?
Bob	There for everyone to see.
Bill	What was?
Bob	Your teeth.
Bill	My teeth?
Bob	Yeah, you remember. Those lumpy bits that protruded from your gums and gnawed away at food and Angela's neck.
Bill	What have my teeth got to do with it?
Bob	*(With emphasis)* They were the token of your affection, the memento of your romantic liaison with Angela.
Bill	Oh.
Bob	Remember now? Apparently you left them with her for safekeeping while you and she were . . .
Bill	Yeah, yeah, we know that bit.
Bob	And she kept them in a jar on the shelf above the fire for years afterwards.

Bill   *(Groans with head in hands)* Oh no, how could she?

Bob   She was very fond of you.

Bill   So it seems.

Bob   *(Pats Bill on shoulder)* Hey, any little bit of affection in your old age shouldn't be sniffed at.

Bill   S'pose not.

Bob   Course not.

Bill   Can't knock it, can you, really?

Bob   Definitely not.

Bill   *(Turns to Bob)* What about you?

Bob   What about me?

Bill   Anything you want to admit to?

Bob   Hey! Sssh, you never know who's listening. *(Looks around nervously)*

Bill   Nothing you'd want to change?

Bob   Bit late now, isn't it?

Bill   Well, what if you could go back and tweak a few things, shuffle the pack in your favour?

Bob   Now you come to mention it, there are one or two things. Now, let me see, there was that time that . . .

A voice interrupts: 'Next!'

Bill	*(Looks around)* Did you hear that?
Bob	*(Waggles finger in ear)* Hear it? It rattled my brain good and proper.
Bill	I suppose we'd better go and see what we have to do now.
Bob	Next stage in the journey, really.
Bill	You could say that. Funny, though.
Bob	What's that?
Bill	This death lark.
Bob	What about it?
Bill	It's something I've tried to put off for years.
Bob	Like kissing the wife?
Bill	*(Shudders)* Don't talk like that around here. Get us thrown out before they listen to what we've got to say.
Bob	*(Jerks head towards direction of voice)* You don't reckon she's in there, do you?
Bill	What on earth would she be doing in there?
Bob	It doesn't bear thinking about.
Bill	If it were left up to me I know where I'd put her. I'd put her where she could see everybody and everybody could hear her. Let them suffer a few years of her tongue-lashing. They'd soon realise what hell was like.

The voice shouts again: 'NEXT!'

Bob	Come on. We'd better go and see if we're wanted.
Bill	They'd better let us in. If they don't I'll give 'em a dose of verbal.
Bob	I bet you would as well. Mind you, you had a good teacher.
Bill	The best, well, the worst if you were on the receiving end.

(Both Bob and Bill walk off stage.)

Reflect

- If we are so wonderfully made, why do we go wrong so often?
- If we criticise how we look, are we criticising God's creation?

Consider

- Is death something to fear?
- If our teeth need fixing we trust a dentist to do it. If our bodies need fixing we trust a doctor to solve the problem. If life seems more than we can handle, do we trust God?

A step further

Take a look at John 14:6-7. Verse 6 is repeated by a lot of people, for all sorts of reasons, but can we really say we know what it means?

It's all far too simple, when life gets messy, for someone to pat us on the head and tell us that Jesus is the answer. Don't you feel like turning to the person who says that and shouting: *'No he isn't!'*

Think about it. It's almost like snapping our fingers whenever we have a problem and expecting God to do all the dirty work. Don't we have a part to play in sorting out the hassle? Let's be honest, the problem most probably exists because of us. If all we had to do was say: 'Jesus is the answer', and the problem was sorted straight away, wouldn't almost the entire world become followers of Jesus? It'd be a neat trick but we'd be the losers.

Jesus said: 'I am the way . . .' in other words, follow me and together we can find our way through the maze of life. 'I am the truth . . .', believe me, together we can do it. And '. . . the life.' I will give you the strength and support to get you through.

Following Jesus is a journey. There are no short cuts and very few simple answers. We don't suddenly wake up and know the answer to every problem in the known universe. Simply by saying that he was the way, Jesus made it very clear that we were starting out on a journey of discovery the precise moment we placed our faith in him. All you need to do is put one foot in front of the other and thank God that you are able to do so.

Time out

Take some time out and find somewhere to be quiet. Consider the following prayer.

Sometimes, God,
I want to scream and shout . . .
at YOU.
It's like I've been walking for so long,
my feet ache,
I'm hungry,
and I'm desperate for something to drink.
I feel like just falling down
flat, horizontal,
and not getting up again,

at least not for a while.
Do you understand what I'm trying to say?
I'm tired, God.
All this,
everything,
everybody,
just seems far too much to cope with.
At times
I feel as if I've got a problem
for every letter of the alphabet,
and some more!
When times are tough,
when I'm hurting,
crying with frustration,
angry at the world and everybody in it,
it would be really neat
to be able to snap my fingers
and say: 'Job done!'
But you know,
and I know,
that if that was all there was to it,
I'd probably find myself in the same mess,
the same hassle,
feeling the same hurt, frustration and anger,
as I did the time before,
and the time before that, and the time before that,
etc., etc., etc., for ever, amen.
Whenever I feel like this, God,
just give me hug,
a smile and a nudge,
and tell me that I'm not on my own.
That together we're a team,
me and you.

Employment

Nice if you can get it

Dougie licked the marmalade off his fingers and settled down to read the daily delivery of junk mail. Although he knew that none of the envelopes would contain anything of interest, Dougie thought it was only fair to give the sender the benefit of the doubt. He carefully placed each envelope on the table and examined the postmark. Then he sorted the envelopes in order of geographical location. The envelope which had travelled the furthest was given priority over those which had travelled the least distance. This, thought Dougie, was the fairest way of dealing with junk mail. If someone in some distant office had taken the time to search for Dougie's address, place the letter in the envelope and launch the entire package into the postal system, then the letter deserved to be given a few seconds of attention. Dougie was aware that most of his mail arrived courtesy of computer-aided technology, but somewhere a human hand had come into contact with his letter and he felt that a sort of human bond existed when he took the time to open the mail and scan its contents. He didn't want to feel that a letter could travel untouched from computer to dustbin without some form of human caress.

Today was different. The alarm had shocked him into consciousness, as planned. That part was normal. The shower had warmed his senses and reminded his body that it was still, partially, alive. That, too, was normal. The problem was the marmalade. It tasted different.

Dougie checked the label. It was the same as usual. He checked his toast. It was the same burnt offering. Dougie sat back in his chair and stroked his chin. Immediately he knew he shouldn't have done the stroking bit.

Apart from a sticky chin (have you noticed, no matter how much you lick your fingers they still feel sticky?), Dougie knew why today was different. He threw the letters and blackened crusts of toast towards the kitchen bin. It was Monday.

Dougie looked out of the kitchen window. It wasn't raining and it should have been. Mondays were miserable so why shouldn't it be raining? What made Dougie feel like a really sad bloke was the fact that he could actually remember the Boomtown Rats song: 'I don't like Mondays'. And, when you think about it, you really can't get much sadder than that.

With an irritation refined over years of enduring Mondays, Dougie mechanically poured the dregs of his coffee into the sink, rinsed the mug under the tap, gave the mug a quick wipe with the tea-towel, and threw it over the back of the chair (*not* the mug, the tea-towel!). Slowly, he shuffled towards the door and prepared himself for the uphill struggle of climbing the stairs to the bathroom.

It wasn't the routine flick of water in the face, or wedging a toothbrush into his mouth that made Dougie feel so miserable, it was purely because the actions all signalled the inevitable, the dreaded moment when he would reluctantly allow each foot to retrace his steps down the stairs and towards the ultimate, the final once and for all (until Tuesday) task of stepping into the brisk morning air and the journey to work.

As he manoeuvred his arms into the jacket reserved for the occasion, Dougie pulled a face in the mirror, made a cursory check of his teeth for any debris that would create unwanted attention, and gave his hair a deft flick. With a sigh worthy of a condemned man, Dougie opened the door to the outside world.

He knew he shouldn't complain. At least he had a job, such as it was. He'd heard, countless times, the reasons why he should be grateful, thankful for what he had, how he should think of the poor and destitute, those who struggled to exist. But, no matter how much he considered every logical, rational reason for being thankful for his job, it didn't make Mondays feel any better. Come to think of it, he felt much the same about Tuesday, Wednesday, Thursday and Friday. You name the day and he felt the same – hours of watching the clock count the monotonous, relentless minutes and seconds of his uneventful existence. Day after day, he tried not to look at the clock, hoping that when he did finally succumb to the inevitable glance time would have gained wings and brought the wretched day to a close. It never worked. It was agony seeing the clock making its casual way through the day, not hurrying for anyone, ignoring the pleading, the insults and jibes, just steadily going about its time-honoured business.

Dougie walked along the street and towards the daily grind. With a shake of his head, he wondered whether he would be walking the same path next year, doing the same things, the same routine? A second shake of the head, accompanied by a sigh, betrayed his thoughts. Would things change? It would take a miracle. With shoulders hunched against the morning air, Dougie walked into the future.

Occupied with being unoccupied

Phil stared at the teapot. It didn't move, so neither did he. After several seconds of stillness had passed into eternity, Phil coerced his body into one major effort, grasped the handle and poured himself another mug of tea.

Wrapping his hands around the warming mug, he stretched his jaw, yawned and began a long sip of the brown liquid. The yawn changed to a sigh as his thoughts meandered around his mind. He knew the cerebral activity wouldn't last too long, there wasn't a lot to think about. Every day was the same: open eye-lids, sniff, blink and allow feet to emerge from under the duvet, closely followed by a pair of legs to rival celery, and a body that wouldn't have looked out of place in a wax museum. The daily routine continued with an inspection of the eyes in the mirror, an amble down the stairs and the first exercise of the day: bending to pick the mail from the floor.

Nonchalantly throwing the mail onto the table, Phil's next move required careful deliberation and a degree of physical co-ordination that had lain dormant for many hours. The careful gauging of the volume of water in the kettle was quickly followed by a decision whether to manoeuvre the kettle under the tap and add more water or take a gamble and connect the kettle to its power source and let physics take its course. The next stage demanded precision. Leaving the kettle to become infused with power, Phil then had to time everything to perfection. If he delayed the process at any point, the kettle will have finished its brief electrical liaison and begin to allow the relationship to cool. If allowed to cool for too long, the results would be disastrous, and the brew would be far from perfect. But, if he hurried any part of the ritual, he would be left waiting, watching the kettle perform its function. It was then a race to see who would reach boiling point first.

However, if everything went according to plan, then Phil could sit and sip in peace, contentment spreading across his face like a summer cloud.

There was never any hurry to sort through the mail. The correspondence rarely varied. With an ability to recog-nise rejection, developed over the years, Phil knew that between the junk mail, offering him an instant solution to all his debt problems, and the congratulatory letter informing him that he had won £10,000 pounds, providing he returned his winning numbers within the next ten days and accepted a trial subscription to a magazine with no obligation, there would be the usual letter thanking him for his application and assuring him that his details would be kept on file for the next six months.

There was never any disguising the fact that these letters were no more and no less a rejection of all that Phil had to offer the economy. In the beginning, he'd become increasingly depressed as each letter 'regretted to inform him . . .'; and finding a job became his personal Holy Grail. Gradually, as time passed, the letters had less impact and the word 'Employment' was nothing more than political rhetoric.

Finally, to make form filling a little more interesting, Phil had become increasingly inventive in his list of qualifications and portrayal of hobbies. No one had ever questioned his Master's degree in Origami or, listed among his countless hobbies, wind-surfing down the Nile and collecting supermarket receipts. This assumed acceptance of his ability encouraged Phil to explore the possibility of becoming the first man to own an allotment on the moon, well, on paper at least.

Phil lifted the lid of the teapot and peered inside. Was there enough of the life-giving liquid left to raise the level in his mug? First impression seemed to imply that there wasn't enough liquid to even discolour the bottom of his mug. He sat back and pondered the eternal question: should he confront the day or make another pot of tea? With a satisfied nod of his head, he stretched his arms, arched his back, sighed and walked over to the kettle with a purposeful smile.

Reflect

- Is work a prison or a place to become the person God might want us to be?
- If work takes up so much of our life, should we try to see what God can do in our life there or simply consider work a necessary evil?

Consider

- Should we feel guilty if we are unemployed?
- How can we make unemployment a positive experience?

A step further

Have a look at 2 Timothy 2:15-16. Work, and even just looking for work, takes up a large part of our waking hours. A lot of people think of work as just something they do, nothing to really bother about, or that it would be great to be able to work in a Christian organisation. The Bible reference encourages us not to be ashamed of what we do, but to do it so that God will be pleased with us.

Jesus says that we are like salt for everyone on earth (see Matthew 5:13). Salt can help bring out the flavour in food and, if left out, wouldn't taste quite the same. We have a part to play wherever we are. We can be a bit of God where we work, a reflection of his love, a voice to be heard.

Time out

It isn't easy sorting out what we think about work. Have a look at the following Bible verses.

Don't be stupid and believe all you hear; be clever and know where you are headed . . . Stupidity leads to foolishness; be clever and learn . . . Hard work is worthwhile, but empty talk will make you poor . . . It's clever to be patient, but it's stupid to lose your temper . . . It's healthy to be content, but envy can eat you up. (Proverbs 14:15, 18, 23, 29, 30)

Greed

The self and nothing but the self

No one really wants to admit to being *greedy*, except when it's the last chocolate digestive biscuit left on the plate! Being *greedy* implies all sorts of negative things, for instance: selfish, grasping, egotistical, a glutton, piggish, and just a touch preoccupied with your own desires.

It isn't easy trying to examine our own motives and desires; it can lead to all sorts of hassle! The two characters in the following sketch consider the concept of greed with all the sensitivity of a house-brick.

Characters	Sam and Don are two labourers on a building site. Both have a sort of tired, seen-it-all, done-it-all and got the T-shirt outlook on life.
Scene	An out-of-the-way corner of a building site. Sam and Don are sitting on milk crates and drinking large mugs of tea. In front of them is a large teapot sitting on a piece of scrap wood, which itself is sitting on a pile of bricks.
Props	Ripped jeans, old T-shirts and scuffed boots for Sam and Don. A couple of milk crates, bricks and a scrap of wood make up the furnishings and a couple of newspapers, mugs and large teapot complete the picture.

Sam   Have you seen this? (*Holds newspaper at arm's length*)

Don   What's that?

Sam   (*Rustles newspaper*) It's a multidimensional communication device whose usefulness has obviously bypassed your lack of intelligence.

Don	*(Takes a swig of tea and then wipes mouth with sleeve)* Has the wife packed you cheese and onion sandwiches again?
Sam	What's it to you?
Don	You're always cranky when she packs you cheese and pickle.
Sam	*(Folds newspaper in half and passes it to Don)* Look here.
Don	*(Squints at newspaper. Reads slowly)* HAMSTER IN CANAL RESCUE DRAMA . . .?
Sam	*(Taps newspaper in agitation)* Not that, you daft prune. *(Taps paper again)* This.
Don	*(Reads slowly)* DUSTBIN LOTTERY. REFUSE-COLLECTORS SCOOP WEEKEND JACKPOT. 'WE'VE *BIN* AND DONE IT', SAYS A DELIGHTED ERIC COUGHMUCK.
Sam	*(Shakes head)* A scandal if ever I heard one.
Don	*(Sniffs)* Good luck to 'em, I say.
Sam	*(Angrily)* Good luck? What do you mean, good luck?
Don	It's what I say, good luck to 'em.
Sam	No luck about it. A downright case of victimisation, I reckon.
Don	You what?
Sam	That's right. Victimisation. Blokes like that shouldn't be allowed to win such enormous amounts of money.
Don	*(Shrugs)* Why's that?

Sam   Cos they'll only go and spend it, that's why.

Don   Oh?

Sam   Yeah, victimisation. Cos it weren't us that won!

Don   *(Grins)* Do I detect a slight aroma of sour grapes?

Sam   Slight aroma? Nothing slight at all. It's a huge great gale, mate.

Don   I still say good luck to 'em.

Sam   You would.

Don   *(Takes a swig of tea and stretches legs)* Too much trouble, mate, if you ask me.

Sam   It ain't too much trouble if you plan it right.

Don   So, you given it some thought, then?

Sam   Course I have, hasn't everybody?

Don   Can't say I've wasted too many seconds of my beauty sleep.

Sam   You're just saying that. I bet you've got a list of all the numbers that have ever been drawn written down somewhere. *(Sits upright, looks at Don and then angrily points a finger at him)* I bet you are trying to see whether there's a pattern or what numbers come up regular like. *(Folds arms and turns head away from Don)* You devious so-and-so.

Don   'Ere, 'ang on a mo. Who the cement and brick dust do you think you're talking to?

(Sam turns slowly towards Don and sniffs haughtily)

Don   What's up with your nose? Has your cheese and pickle upset your innards? *(Picks up mug of tea and takes a swig)*

Sam   *(Spoken in a comic posh voice)* Nothin' wrong with my digestive system, thank you very much. If there is an unwelcome aroma around here, I do believe that you should manoeuvre your olfactory equipment somewhere around your vicinity.

Don   *(Pauses drinking with mug poised at mouth. Slowly, he places mug onto the table)* Don't you talk to me in that tone of voice and use such disgusting language.

Sam   *(Picks up his own mug of tea)* For your information, olfactory is to do with smelling.

Don   *(Rocks head from side to side in a mocking manner)* Oooh! So who's been reading the back of the cereal packet again?

Sam   *(Puts his mug onto the table, picks up the paper and places it directly in front of his face. He speaks to Don from behind the paper)* If you can't talk properly, there's no point in talking at all.

(Don picks up his newspaper and places it directly in front of his face. A few seconds of silence take place, only interrupted by the sound of rustling newspapers)

Don   *(Peers around edge of his newspaper)* Read anything interesting?

Sam   Who's asking?

Don   Me, you great barn-pot.

Sam   *(Still speaking from behind newspaper)* One or two articles which stimulate the cerebral thinking tackle.

Don   *(Folds newspaper and places it onto the table)* Wonder what they're going to do with it all.

Sam   *(Places newspaper onto the table and leans forward, talking excitedly)* Exactly! Just what I was thinking. What are they going to do with it all?

Don   The mind boggles.

Sam   And so it should. All that money going to waste.

Don   Hmm. You may be right there. It's difficult to imagine that they would spend it carefully, you know, put the money where it'll do the most good.

Sam   I can't see it being any good them sticking it into a high-interest account; the money wouldn't be in there long enough.

Don   No, I wasn't thinking of them saving it.

Sam   Neither were they!

Don   Possibly true. But I was thinking more about what good the money would do.

Sam   Precisely, what good would the money do them? Totally the wrong type of people to have such a weight of responsibility hanging over their wallet. Much better off if they gave it all to . . . me!

Don	And exactly what good would *that* do?
Sam	It'd take the worry off their shoulders for a start.
Don	And having all that money wouldn't make you worry?
Sam	Definitely not! There's so many good uses I could put the money to.
Don	Such as?
Sam	*(Ponders for a few seconds, stroking chin)* Well . . . there's a really smart sporty number just down the road, lovely curves and . . .
Don	*(Interrupts quickly)* Forget it, she's married.
Sam	Trust you to say that. No, that little red sports car down at the showroom. Good price it is, too.
Don	I bet it is. Enough money to feed a family for a year.
Sam	At least. Anyway, I could always treat her indoors to a new kitchen, you know, all fancy gadgets, gizmos and a pair of rubber gloves.
Don	Rubber gloves? No dishwasher, then?
Sam	*(Look of alarm)* Steady, steady. You can't go mad all at once.
Don	No, that wouldn't do at all. Much better to degenerate slowly into a pitiful wreck.
Sam	Nothing pitiful about it. But there's no point in worrying yourself about money. And, even more important, you don't want to go and stick your money in a bank where other people have to worry about it.

Don	Isn't that what you pay bank charges for, so that they can worry about your money?
Sam	Look, mate. Just because you have money doesn't mean that you have to ignore the feelings and needs of your fellow human beings.
Don	Yeah, just what I meant earlier. Just think what you could do with all that money.
Sam	*(Nods enthusiastically)* I am, mate, I am.
Don	*(Shakes head)* No, what I mean is, why should just a few people have all that money when it could be spread about a bit, do some good in lots of places?
Sam	*(Leaning forward in agitation)* Hey! Hang about a minute. Listen to what I'm saying. You can't go giving money away willy-nilly. Cause more harm than good. Those who haven't got money get used to being without it. A bit of what you ain't had you can't grieve about, see?
Don	Er, sort of.
Sam	And, those who are used to dealing with money are the best people to have money, right?
Don	And so where does that leave us?
Sam	In desperate need of lots of money cos I can't get used to having none and I don't want to get used to having none either!
Don	Oh, right. But doesn't that contradict what you've just been saying about those that have are the best placed to deal with it, sort of thing?

Sam	Not at all. I ain't got enough cos I spends it as soon as I get it, see? So, I know how to use this 'ere money and I need more to show that I know what I'm doing, OK?
Don	And it ain't right that two people, who really don't know how to use money correctly, should win such enormous great lumps of the folding stuff?
Sam	Couldn't put it neater myself.
Don	*(Leans forward and lifts the teapot ready to pour)* Want another wetting?
Sam	Wouldn't say no to that, my friend. Why have one when three's so much better?
Don	*(Nods head)* Exactly. *(Passes mug to Sam)* Chin up, slurp up and let's get to work.
Sam	*(Lifts mug)* Cheers. Here's more power to my wallet, eh?
Don	*(Lifts mug)* Yeah, cheers and lots of the folding stuff.

Give a little bit?

Most of us like to think that we are naturally generous. We might stand in front of the mirror and say: 'Mirror, mirror, on the wall. Who is the most generous of them all?' After a few moments, and on hearing the mirror's response we just then might be heard to say: 'Hey! Where's my name amongst all those?'

Rather than rely on temperamental mirrors, why not check out your generosity rating with the following quiz?

Choose one response, from a choice of three, which best describes how you would normally react to the situation.

1. You have just one chocolate-coated toffee left. Your best mate is finding it difficult not to drool. Do you:
   a. Unwrap the sweet, smile nicely, and pop it into your mouth?
   b. Unwrap the sweet and offer it to your mate?
   c. Unwrap the sweet, pop it into your mouth and, when you have sucked all the chocolate off, offer the remaining toffee to your mate?

2. You have just eaten four jam doughnuts. There is one left in the bag. Do you:
   a. Offer the remaining doughnut to anyone who's feeling deprived of jam?
   b. Throw the remaining doughnut into the waste-bin (just so that you're not tempted to eat it and make yourself sick)?
   c. Wrap the doughnut in the bag and keep it for later?

3. You're driving home late at night. There's a gale-force wind and the rain is lashing against your windscreen faster than the wiper-blades can do their business. Just ahead of you someone is waiting to cross the road. Do you:
   a. Slow down and allow them to cross over the road?
   b. Look for a puddle near the pedestrian, and drive through it at speed?
   c. Stop the car and offer the person a lift?

4. Your brother has borrowed your favourite T-shirt to wear while he plays football. When he finally remembers to return it to you it's covered in mud. Do you:
   a. Ask for an apology and extract a promise from him never to borrow your clothes again?

b. Tell him it's OK as long as he washes the T-shirt?

c. Smile sweetly and later pour a bucket of mud into his bed?

5. The film has just finished on TV. The rest of the family are busily scanning the newspaper to find out what programmes are on the other TV channels. The programme you want to watch is immediately after the film and on the same channel. Do you:

   a. Ask what programme the rest of the family have agreed to watch?

   b. Hide the remote control under the chair?

   c. Suggest that the family place the names of all the programmes into a bag, with the one drawn out being the one everybody watches?

6. You're walking along the High Street with only a pound coin in your pocket. Not far away from you stands a guy selling the *Big Issue*. Do you:

   a. Buy a copy of the *Big Issue*?

   b. Buy two cups of coffee from a takeaway, and offer one to the guy?

   c. Walk into the nearest shop and see what you can buy with your money?

7. It's Christmas and you've been given two identical presents. Do you:

   a. Put one of the presents in a cupboard and use it as a gift for someone's birthday?

   b. Take it to a charity shop?

   c. Put it away safely until the other one has worn out?

8. You are eating a meal with your relatives. In front of you is a huge mound of brussels sprouts, and the thought of eating them makes your stomach feel like a washing-machine on the spin cycle. Do you:

    a. Smile weakly, cover the offending green blobs in tomato ketchup, place one in your mouth and think about other notable martyrs?

    b. Make gagging noises and run to the toilet?

    c. Bury them in mashed potato and hope no one notices?

9. You've got a streaming cold and you haven't stopped wiping your nose since breakfast. Your best mate has just started sneezing and cannot find anything to wipe their nose with. A quick check of your pocket reveals that you only have one clean tissue left to use. Do you:

    a. Suggest that your friend use their sleeve to wipe their nose?

    b. Offer them one of your used tissues?

    c. Give them your last clean tissue?

10. You've just managed to get to the Summer Fair for the final thirty minutes of the event. Everyone appears to have had a good time and a lot of money has been raised for charity. Your favourite 'game', throwing a cold, wet sponge at someone's face, is just closing. You're desperate to have a go with the sponge even though the 'volunteer' is complaining of being extremely cold and totally wet through. Do you:

    a. Pay your money and throw the sponge so that it only just hits the target?

    b. Pay your money without throwing a sponge?

    c. Pay your money and throw as many sponges as you can at the target?

Find your total score using the following answer guide:

1. a = 0	b = 2	c = 1	4. a = 1	b = 2	c = 0
2. a = 2	b = 0	c = 1	5. a = 2	b = 0	c = 1
3. a = 1	b = 0	c = 2	6. a = 2	b = 1	c = 0

7. a = 1   b = 2   c = 0   9. a = 0   b = 1   c = 2
8. a = 2   b = 0   c = 1   10. a = 1   b = 2   c = 0

Add your total points scored together and discover how you rate in the generosity stakes.

15-20 points
You really are a bit too good to be true! In fact, a real smoothie in playing the generosity game. Don't you think you may be overdoing it a bit? The problem with being *this* nice, is that almost everyone will be watching your every move, just waiting for you to do something, anything, that they can use to point the finger and say they knew you were being too sweet to hide your sour side! Give yourself, and other people, a break. Treat yourself to that last chocolate and enjoy it!

6-14 points
You seem to play a balancing game. Depending on your mood you tread a fine line between greed and generosity. It can appear, to the casual observer, that you behave in a more calculated way than being spontaneous in your actions. Rather than behave in an irrational manner, you tend to think about your actions and what consequences they may have. Although you may be swayed by the emotional tug of the rattled collecting box or TV advert for charitable causes, you prefer to plan the way you give rather than respond to any, and every, good cause.

0-5 points
Hmm, not a score to shout about. It seems obvious that the most important consideration for your behaviour is . . . yourself! Although you recognise what other people may need, you're just thankful that you've managed to acquire what you need for a comfortable life and don't want to jeopardise your way of life by acting with any semblance of generosity. The only problem with this type

of thinking is that other people are likely to respond to you in the same way that you responded to them.

Reflect

- Is gambling, whether playing the lottery or at the casino, being greedy?
- Why is it that often, the more we have, the more we want?

Consider

- Who is the greediest, the one who grabs what they can or the one who constantly wishes they had more?
- Does having what we want make us any happier?

A step further

Have a glance at Matthew 6:19-21. This Bible reference is often used to suggest that Jesus encouraged people to live in poverty and not to plan for the future. To use it in this way is to totally miss the point of what Jesus was saying. Jesus was far more concerned with a person's heart attitude than whether they have money or not.

If your desire is to be wealthy, or wealthier, then it is that which will be your driving force. That desire will become the main focus for your existence. All Jesus is saying is that it's not a problem to have money, but why use so much energy chasing after something that either wears out or becomes unfashionable? More importantly, whatever you possess is earth-bound; you can't take it with you, as they say!

Everyone sets their hearts on what they believe to be important, and it's this that influences and motivates their lives. Jesus suggests that having God as our focus helps us to get things into perspective. It's not so much having as what we do with it that counts.

Time out

Find a place where you won't be disturbed and read the
following prayer:

Just think, Lord,
what I could do with all that money.
You know,
if I won the lottery.
Or should I say, when I win the lottery,
you know, with a bit of help from you know who!
Now, come on,
you did say you'd take care of everything,
didn't you?
And, with all that extra folding money
just think what I could do.
I've been giving it a lot of thought, you know,
it's a kind of dream of mine,
well, a constant stream of images, really,
zinging through my brain.
There's so many countries I haven't been to,
so many places that my feet haven't trod.
There's so many things I haven't done,
like bungee-jumping from the San Francisco bridge,
or abseiling down the pyramids or
white-water rafting down the Grand Canyon.
I even fancy penguin spotting in Antarctica,
and scuba diving in the Grand Union Canal.
I've got my eye on a rather nice sporty number
and I quite fancy a Porsche as well.
I could do with a few new clothes
just to make my wardrobe feel useful.
I've never eaten in those really posh restaurants
or sipped champagne
from a wellington boot.
All these things I want to do, Lord.
Just think what I could do.
Pardon?

Excuse me?
You have thought of what I would do?
And?
Oh.
Hmm. I did forget one or two things,
or should I say lots of things
and people, and stuff.
Just one more thing,
I don't remember
including you
in all my plans
and schemes
and things.
Er . . .

Emotions _____

The power of . . .

What on earth is *love* about? Wouldn't life be just a little bit easier, if we didn't have to worry about *love*? Let's face it, when we're in *love* we worry about doing or saying the wrong thing, acting stupid or constantly pretending to be someone different from who we really are. And, when we're not in *love*, we spend enormous amounts of time worrying about it.

Whether we're in love or not, it affects our thinking, our emotions and dictates the way we behave (it also costs a fortune in text messages!).

Take the average person who has just spotted someone they would like to share a plate of spaghetti with. Here's a checklist of some of the questions, physical anomalies and dodgy behaviour that might occur:

Thinking
1. What time is it?
2. How do you make spaghetti?
3. When did I last clean my teeth?
4. Who cares what time it is?
5. Forget the spaghetti. I'll get a takeaway.
6. Should I try to impress them with my juggling pickled gherkins trick?
7. What am I doing here?

Emotions
1. Body temperature rises by 50 per cent.
2. Grins at anything and everybody.
3. The sun always seems to be shining.
4. Every thought becomes poetry, as the last word of each sentence rhymes.
5. Dreams seem to feature lots of boats on lakes, tall

grass swaying in the breeze, with every scene accompanied by the sounds of a string orchestra.
6. Time spent apart appears to be going backwards, while time together seems to be double speed.
7. Your stomach seems to be inhabited by butterflies.

Behaviour
1. Humming while doing the washing-up.
2. Collecting travel brochures featuring exotic locations.
3. Buying a CD compilation entitled: 'Hits for lovers'.
4. Stopping to check your appearance in any reflective surface.
5. Spraying deodorant in trainers.
6. Restricting food intake to raspberry jelly and digestive biscuits.
7. Gazing in the florist's window.

If you can relate to any three out of each of the above categories then, and please make sure that you're already sitting down, or have a pile of cushions behind you – you have contracted, potentially one of the most anti-social conditions known to humankind . . . *love*!

Hang on a moment, it can't be as bad as that, can it? Well, it's not; if you think walking around in a semi-comatose state, dribbling profusely, and grinning whenever anybody asks you a question is socially acceptable, then possibly, just possibly, it's not quite as bad as all that.

Let's take a few steps back. If love consists entirely of behaving in strange ways, and responding to everyone as if you're in a trance, then, sooner or later, someone may take you to one side and offer a few suggestions (possibly reinforced with a piece of wet fish wrapped around your head). What happens when the initial feelings of bliss fade, and you can't afford to keep buying flowers, sherbet dips and you've acquired an enormous blister on your finger after continuously typing text messages on your mobile phone for the last three weeks? Now comes the tricky bit.

The trouble with *love* is, it's not like learning algebra, is it? Although it can be a bit like gardening. At first, you get all excited about seeing the plants, you lovingly water them, give them lots of tender loving care and stand back to see what happens. Then comes a tingling down your spine as the plants begin to bloom and put on a display of colour that makes other people turn and stare. Now, here's where things can go one of two ways. Either you continue with the tender loving care, giving the plant all the attention it needs to flourish, or you become bored, tired of seeing the same thing day after day. You forget to water the plant, ignore the little tell-tale signs of neglect, pay far too much attention to other plants, and then, suddenly, what once captivated you and gave you that rush of excitement just thinking about it, has now withered, gone. Your face says it all. Why? What did I do wrong?

The truth slowly creeps into your consciousness. You push it aside, not wanting to acknowledge the reality of your action, or rather, inaction. You spend ages trying to justify your behaviour. Loads of excuses fill your mind in an attempt to put a blanket over the real cause of the abrupt end to your relationship. You occupy yourself with little jobs, get armfuls of books out of the library, anything to distract your mind. But, just as you close your eyes and begin to drift into sleep's warm embrace, a fragment of a memory gradually comes into focus. A feeling of guilt, or a snarl of irritation? Do you tell yourself it would never have worked anyway? Do you try to convince yourself that it was never your fault? There must have been something wrong to start with? Was it really love in the first place?

Facing the truth is never easy. Anyway, isn't being truthful one of the many characteristics of love? Love goes through phases. After the initial stages of unseemly behaviour (kissing in the supermarket, touching hands in the freezer section, gazing into each other's eyes at the checkout), the attraction explores other aspects of your character. You begin to develop an understanding of each other. You notice each other's likes and dislikes, how many spoons of sugar they have in their cup of tea and, on occasions, talk to each other! It's a journey of exploration, of understanding, of getting on each other's nerves and appreciating why. It's getting really annoyed that your partner doesn't agree with you on everything! It's an understanding that love is looking in the same direction, even though your interpretation of the view may differ.

You could say that love is like looking at a diamond. It has many facets, each reflecting something of its surroundings. It is admired, valued and something that everyone wants. As a raw, uncut diamond, fresh from the ground, it already has all the qualities of the finished product. It needs careful handling, it requires someone to see its value, to gently coax it into shape, and finally, apply the finishing touches that make it instantly identifiable as a thing of beauty.

Just as a diamond will shine out from a pile of stones, so will love shine out from its surroundings. It's special, a thing to hold on to, something to admire, value and want for yourself.

So, just what is love? Is it merely a commodity that can be bought, traded or hidden away from prying eyes? Surely not? Take a step back from the knotted stomach, the vacant expression and gooey behaviour. Love is a gift. A gift that's given freely because the whole heart and mind is set on that one purpose: to love and be loved. And, like a diamond, it can reflect many things. It's something that is precious and which means everything to those who share it. Again, as a diamond, love is many faceted. It has different sides. It is not just one expression, but a reflection of many forms and shades. It's not always easy to form. It's often far harder than we imagine. It's something that requires patience and determination. Sometimes it's hard graft, at other times it's a pleasure. But the whole process is worth every bit of effort. Love is something that everyone can admire and appreciate. Although love is a gift to each other, it is also something that needs to be seen, brought into the light so that everyone can see its reflected beauty.

A hatful of hate

H: Hostage

Held to ransom. Altered. Taken from a secure environment and hidden. Dark. Cannot see. Concealed. Shrouded from inquisitive eyes. A myriad thoughts permeate the darkness.

Uncertainty. Afraid. Fear. A chilled spine. The unknown becomes familiar. A tenuous link to reality. What? Why? Where? Shout. No one hears, or, if they hear, they don't respond.

Alone. Feelings of betrayal. Cold, cold thoughts chill the atmosphere. Muscles ache. Head hurts. Numb emotions. Can't understand. How could this happen?

Time passes. Difficult to estimate how long. Permanent darkness. Flashes of memories play against a black backdrop. Sounds are muffled. Unclear. Snatches of conversations appear out of syncopation. Disjointed. A remnant from the past.

Freedom. What is freedom? Isn't it relative? Is one person's freedom another person's idea of captivity? Is freedom movement? The ability to go from one place to another through choice? Could freedom be the opportunity to behave differently? To behave without criticism? To allow the individual expression of life to be on permanent exhibition?

Waiting. Forever waiting. Feeling violated. Mentally abused. Unable to express emotions. Restricted. Wanting to flex muscles. Feelings of anger building inside. Wanting to hit out, hurt, injure. Make someone else feel the same. How would they like to feel this way?

Hostage to your own thoughts. Bound by invisible threads. Held captive by the struggle between right and wrong. Black and white. Ensnared by the greyness of indecision, the lack of judgement, care, empathy. Feelings of self-worth submerged under a sea of guilt. Self-worth? Is self-worth for an individual, or every individual?

Hostage. A slave to self? Enslaved by the idea of putting personal desires, wants, dreams before that of liberty? Are the chains that bind of our own making? Does the pursuit of a dream, or desire, ignore the liberty of other people? Does the end justify the means? Does nothing matter in the race for achievement?

The feelings that drive towards reaching the destination, can become as strong as any chains made by human hands. The urge to justify an existence can trample another person's right to exist, to be free. To achieve one freedom can result in captivity for someone else. The drive to own, to have and to hold, can be the force by which another person loses the little they have. The urge to have what we want, when we want it, are the chains that can hold each person hostage to their desire. The chains of desire are also the chains that force other people to become hostages to poverty. Cause and effect.

A: Anger

You know *that* feeling all too well. It starts with a momentary flicker of the eyelid, then a quick swallow while a few neurons stir in your brain, as a grey mist clouds your vision (and your judgement).

Within milliseconds, your temperature has risen several notches on the thermometer, and a hot, prickling sensation has begun to irritate you even further. To make matters worse, a red hue has coloured every visible part of your body. Without a shadow of doubt, you're ANGRY.

At that precise moment of heated exchange, the question 'Why?' is submerged under a pile of indignation and amazement that anyone had the sheer nerve to disagree with you!

Accepting the fact that anyone has a different opinion, or perspective, is about as easy as saying that a Party Political Broadcast is essential viewing. Someone having a different opinion or perspective, shouldn't be a problem. Getting angry because someone chooses to be different *is* a problem.

Being angry simply means having an intense sense of displeasure. It's the opposite of having pleasure, of being at ease or comfortable. But the question is, why are we angry, uncomfortable or displeased about something?

Perhaps there should be an 'Anger' scale, similar to a 'Richter' used for measuring the intensity of an earthquake. For example:

Level 1: The bathroom door is locked.

Level 2: The bathroom door is still locked!

Level 3: The bus is late.

Level 4: The bus drives straight past you.

Level 5: You discover a small stain on your jeans.

Level 6: Rubbing the stain with a wet cloth has made the stain larger.

Level 7: That spot on your chin is *still* there.

Level 8: There are three spots on your chin.

Level 9: It's pasta again for tea.

Level 10: Being made to stay until you've eaten all your pasta.

You could devise your own 'Anger' scale and possibly come up with a list different from mine and, more than likely, have twenty levels!

Many things can make us feel so angry that we want to chew somebody's ear or, given the scarcity of available ears when things go critical, thump something (or someone!). The urge to do something is almost overwhelming. Just standing still, give or take the odd seismic tremor, only seems to make matters worse. Your imagination goes into overdrive, the palms of your hands drip buckets and your face burns with indignation. Until . . . well, you know how it is, the only thing that's going to make you feel better is pouring a cold mug of drinking chocolate over *that* person's feet, squeezing a doughnut so hard that the jam oozes between your fingers, and then rubbing your jam-flavoured hand through *that* person's hair and telling them *'it's all right now, I feel so much better!'* It's almost that the person with the newly created jam-styled hair will have something to say about your attempts at styling, and what they say may not quite square-up with your perspective on matters!

It all seems to be a matter of cause and effect, action and reaction, the vicious circle of verbal conflict, physical contact and verbal conflict. Even when you're on your own things can go completely pear-shaped. There doesn't need to be any outside intervention to your fragile state of being. It all happens quite simply. One moment you're enjoying sipping a quiet cup of tea, a momentary lapse of concentration and you're swimming in a chair full of hot tea. Jumping out of your seat you knock the biscuit jar onto the floor, breaking it into a thousand shards of toe-damaging debris and biscuit crumbs. In an attempt to avoid severe lacerations of the foot, you leap over the mess and, mid-flight, dislodge a pot-plant which then disgorges its entire contents over the coffee table. Angrily you make a grab for the vacuum cleaner and swing it into action only to succeed in pulling the electric plug out of the socket which, in turn, finds you being smacked in the mouth by a flying plug.

With no attempt at sane behaviour, you charge across the room and kick the kitchen door. After a two-hour wait at the local hospital's accident and emergency department, the nurse applies a bandage to your badly bruised toes and suggests that you indulge in some less physical exercise. All that for a cup of tea? Anyway, it was your third cup of tea in ten minutes!

Was it worth it? As one thing leads to another, a misplaced outburst can quickly find us on the slippery slope to humiliation. Is anger similar to holding a box of matches in a firework factory, the potential to do a vast amount of destruction or, if used carefully, the essential ingredient to cause an explosive display which will make people sit up and watch?

T: Terror

Have we any idea what it is like to live in *terror*? Do we even have an inkling what the word means? Terror: to live in extreme fear, dread, alarm, anxiety, horror and panic. We can watch terror from the security of an armchair. The images flicker into our short-term memories and are then ejected as a trivial news item occupies our senses. We can turn terror on and off. We can choose to watch a fictionalised image of terror whenever we go to the video store. The pictures can make us shudder, gasp in horror, feel frightened and uncomfortable, but we're safe in the knowledge that it isn't real, at least, not for us.

We can switch off the terror, distance ourselves from the harsh reality of walking a precipice in the darkness. Other people's terror is the stuff of their nightmares, not ours. We're safe, comfortable, assured of our place in society, our statutory rights as written on every guarantee for consumer products.

An American psychologist, Abraham Maslow, suggested that there were five distinct types of human needs which could be related hierarchically. The five needs, in order of importance were:

- Survival: air, food and drink, shelter.
- Safety: safety, security, stability and lack of threats.
- Social: belonging, affection and love.
- Esteem: recognition and respect from others.
- Self-actualisation: fulfilment, realisation of potential.

Each of the needs requires satisfying. However, the first two needs, the physical considerations, are considered to be basic human rights. The third and fourth needs are essential for our psychological well-being, while the final need can, usually, only be achieved once each of the other four needs are satisfied to a certain degree.

It may be a clichéd phrase, but most of the five human needs are *'taken for granted'*. We expect to have air to breathe, food and shelter, to be able to walk freely along any street without fear of losing our freedom or life. It's not too much to expect, is it?

But is there ever a moment of time, a snatch of consciousness, that makes us question what we so often accept as *normal*? Do you ever wonder what it would be like to live in constant fear, to dread the sound of footsteps echoing in the night air? Have you ever dreamt of someone chasing you, your feet feel like lumps of clay, your lungs feel as if they're at bursting point, no matter which way you turn your pursuer seems to be guessing your every move?

Terror is an emotion that is commonplace to many people. They live in fear of that fateful knock at the door, the crash of woodwork as the unanswered knock is followed by a violent intrusion. Sometimes people are terrorised because of their race, colour or belief. Verbal abuse, physical violence, threats, paint daubed on walls by unknown hands who articulate violence. Terror parades in many guises and can be indiscriminate in its discrimination.

It isn't until we lose something that we recognise its value. Often, we are so preoccupied with things that may seem vital to us, things that we've wanted for so long and, when we've got them, are so careful not to lose or damage, that we can overlook what is really important. It is also far too easy to ignore the cries of those who have lost their basic freedom, those who live in terror, fear, dread. We can switch off, they are unable to escape. If we ignore the cries that scream for our attention, will there be ears to hear our screams?

E: Envy

It's a bit embarrassing really. I didn't mean to get caught staring. You know how it is, a quick glance soon becomes a prolonged stare. It was apparent to everybody what I was doing, but it wasn't until my dribble had formed an Olympic-sized swimming pool on the table that I became aware of being watched myself. After that, the itchy, prickly heat that embraced my neck and face was hot enough to toast a loaf.

If I'd realised that my behaviour was going to give other people hours of amusement at my expense, I wouldn't have looked in the first place.

I suppose you're wondering what I'm on about. Well, it's quite simple really. But first, you have to understand that I wasn't all 'eyes on stalks' because of some gorgeous creature who happened to pass in front of my eyeballs. It wasn't quite as simple as that. It was the coat. Yeah, the coat. I know, you may think I'm a really sad piece of fish, but I've had my eyes on *that* coat for ages. I've dreamed about *that* coat, I've ogled at it through the shop window, I've even been into the shop and tried the coat on for size, a perfect fit. The down side is, I can't afford it.

It's not just any coat. It's *the* coat of all coats. It's the coat *I* want. I won't be sidetracked by other bits of rag with labels in them. I know what I want and that's it. Well, it was, until the coat walked in draped all over someone else.

If looks could have killed, they would've done, without damaging the coat, you understand. The scowl on my face made my thoughts as clear as a tabloid headline. It was obvious to the world and the line-dancing fraternity just what was going on in my head. Why? Why should someone else be wearing the coat that I wanted? Is there no justice in the world?

To say I was jealous is like saying you could hear a sneeze in an avalanche. One word could not begin to describe how I feel. I'm furious.

Reflect

• Is it possible to avoid conflict?
• Are there any circumstances where hatred can be justified?

Consider

• Does *love* mean always saying sorry?
• Is *love* something we feel or can it be learnt?

A step further

Take a look at Luke 6:27-42. Phew, what a way to live! The picture in verse 41 is hilarious. You can just imagine using a tiny hanky to dab a speck of dust out of your friend's eye while you continually smash them around the head with the log that's protruding from your eye!

As the tears of laughter dry up, the truth of the image hits home. Before we start to accuse other people of dodgy behaviour, we must first take a long, hard look at ourselves. Are we so blameless?

Time out

Try to find somewhere quiet to sit. Perhaps light a candle and focus on the flame for a few moments. Jesus wasn't trying to make us feel continually guilty or cause us to become totally preoccupied with our behaviour. There are two points that he was eager to make. Firstly, think before you act or speak. It may be a cliché, but those who live in a glasshouse shouldn't get into the habit of throwing stones! In other words, don't act all high and mighty and accuse somebody of misbehaving when it's quite obvious to the rest of the known world that we aren't angels ourselves.

Secondly, Jesus wants us to listen to what he's saying, take it to heart and live it out! Far from easy, but if we are genuine in our attempts to behave as Jesus wants us to then we can't be accused of being hypocrites.

Have a look at Proverbs 3:27-32:

Do all you can for everyone who deserves your help. Don't tell your neighbour to come back tomorrow, if you can help today. Don't try to be mean to neighbours who trust you. Don't argue just to be arguing, when you haven't been hurt. Don't be jealous of cruel people or follow their example. The Lord doesn't like anyone who is dishonest, but he lets good people be his friends.

Relationships _____

The mobile phone companies love it. Lots of people love it. Teachers hate it. Parents despair. The normal hum of chatter has almost been replaced by the bleeps and clicks of text-messaging. The exploration of the Amazon is interrupted by the noise of fingers busily tapping at key-pads. These geography lessons cannot compete with the delights of a text message that tells of last night's meeting of him out of Snozzer's class and her from Tufty's class.

Even TV fades into insignificance when the beep of an incoming text-message interrupts life on the sofa. Eyes are held in rapt attention as the stunted words flicker across the small viewing area of the phone. At the last full-stop (a rare use of punctuation), fingers immediately scurry across the key-pad in reply.

You might argue that all communication is good communication. Unfortunately, there are many people who hate and loathe the intrusion of the miniature mobile service. Sometimes it allows things to be said that wouldn't normally be spoken face-to-face. And that's ignoring the ingenious use of language that not only limits the cost of text messages, but limits the use of everything an English teacher loves!

Making up

Text message from Sal.
Wot R U doin 2nite?

Reply from Gaz.
Wot R U doin?

Sal	Dunno
Gaz	FanC goin out?
Sal	mayB

Gaz	R U F2T
Sal	:-)
Gaz	GR8
Sal	N E ideas?
Gaz	D U FanC C in a pic?
Sal	mayB
Gaz	RUOK?
Sal	mayB
Gaz	Wot?
Sal	U were a :@) 2 me
Gaz	never
Sal	were
Gaz	how?
Sal	U XXX Bev
Gaz	How?
Sal	If u don't know how, wot were yur lips doin wiv hers? NEway, I saw U
Gaz	U weren't ment to C. Sorry
Sal	Y?
Gaz	Dunno
Sal	I wan2 hit U where it hurts
Gaz	Gr8
Sal	wot?
Gaz	Nowt
Sal	Say sommat
Gaz	Like wot?
Sal	Like Y?
Gaz	Nowt 2 tell
Sal	Y not say sorry b4 asking 4 a date
Gaz	oops
Sal	Yes oops big time

Gaz	thot U mite not find out
Sal	fat lot U thot
Gaz	it ment nowt
Sal	tell that 2 Bev
Gaz	not poss
Sal	Y?
Gaz	she 8s me
Sal	brill
Gaz	got some1 else
Sal	gr8 U got dumped
Gaz	not
Sal	did
Gaz	Thnq Vmuch
Sal	Welcome. U wanna save money
Gaz	Wot?
Sal	Get off the phone
Gaz	Talk…please
Sal	Go on then
Gaz	Luk. Can we start again
Sal	And let U XXX Bev Bhind my back?
Gaz	No
Sal	Wot. XXX her so that I can C U?
Gaz	No
Sal	Wot then?
Gaz	I wont stra
Sal	U R joking
Gaz	Mean it
Sal	Prove it
Gaz	Wot R U trying to say?
Sal	Can I trust U?

Gaz	Try me. Pls
Sal	??????
Gaz	Wot?
Sal	Thinkin
Gaz	Wots to think about?
Sal	U Tell me
Gaz	I wanna XXX U
Sal	Like Bev?
Gaz	No. Like me and U
Sal	U got a better chance of XXXing roadkill
Gaz	Would it make U change UR mind?
Sal	Poss
Gaz	As long as I wiped my mouth after?
Sal	U always did have style
Gaz	Thnx
Sal	U R welcome
Gaz	So?
Sal	So wot?
Gaz	Can we start again?
Sal	Pls
Gaz	Gr8
Sal	CU tonite?
Gaz	Luv 2
Sal	Time?
Gaz	ASAP
Sal	Gr8
Gaz	Gr8 x2

Breaking up

Confronting someone face to face is never very easy. Using a text-message or, to use its proper name Short

Message Service (SMS), gives you the opportunity to say things you wouldn't normally say without standing behind bullet-proof glass wearing protective goggles and ear muffs.

Text message from Rob:
R U F2T?

Text message from Sarah
?

Rob	R U ?
Sarah	Poss
Rob	xoxoxoxox
Sarah	Wot R they 4?
Rob	Luv U
Sarah	:-o
Rob	Wots rong?
Sarah	U tell me.
Rob	Is it summat I sed?
Sarah	No
Rob	Is it summat I did or didn't do?
Sarah	No
Rob	Wot then?
Sarah	It's U.
Rob	Me?
Sarah	Yes U.
Rob	R U OK?
Sarah	I'm fine.
Rob	So wots rong?
Sarah	Me and U
Rob	Wot R U trying to say?
Sarah	I'm OK we R not.
Rob	O.

Sarah	Yeah O.
Rob	Wanna talk?
Sarah	Not really.
Rob	Tell me what's rong.
Sarah	Life.
Rob	We can change that 2gether.
Sarah	Can't.
Rob	Can.
Sarah	The prob is us, we 2, me and U. get it?
Rob	Still don't understand.
Sarah	U must have rhino skin.
Rob	Why?
Sarah	U don't want to understand or can't.
Rob	Tek your pik.
Sarah	U wanna simple msg?
Rob	Yes. Easy on the big words.
Sarah	Me + U end OK?
Rob	Is this a mob dump?
Sarah	Yes.
Rob	Y?
Sarah	Bcos.
Rob	Is there NE1 else?
Sarah	No.
Rob	NO1.
Sarah	NO1 at all.
Rob	Y end then?
Sarah	Bcos I've had enuff.
Rob	Of wot?
Sarah	U OK?
Rob	Suppose so.

Sarah	Can we end msg? Cost=mega bucks.
Rob	CU L8R?
Sarah	Sometime never OK?
Rob	Last word?
Sarah	Def.
Rob	R U sure?
Rob	LO Sarah?
Rob	NE1 there?
Rob	PCM
Rob	Ello?

Reflect

- Why are relationships so difficult?
- Should we feel guilty if our relationship gets awkward at times?

Consider

- Do difficult times make or break a relationship?
- Is saying 'sorry' a sign of weakness?

A step further

There are a lot of references in the Bible about relationships. Simply being attracted to another person is only the start of a relationship, the hard work is just about to begin.

The Bible encourages us to look beyond the 'wow' factor, and see the whole person. For instance, in Proverbs 31:30, we read that 'Charm can be deceiving, and beauty fades away, but a woman who honours the Lord deserves to be praised.' The cliché 'beauty is only skin deep' rings true, particularly when gravity gets the better of us and the wrinkles take over.

Relationships are often tough. There are no easy answers and certainly no 'Duffer's guide to relationships'. The straightforward, simple truth is that a successful relationship is often built on a foundation of rubble. The rubble is the debris left over when selfishness and pride have given way to honesty and forgiveness. If you can't be honest with another person, and have the bottle to say sorry, then you're facing a slap in the face when the love of your life (well, at least for the last few hours), tells you just what they think of you and slam the door.

How long you can stand a see-saw relationship depends on how much you want to do what's right. Being honest means being up-front with yourself, with your partner and with God. If you can face all three with a smile then you're on the right track.

Time out

Try to find a place where you won't be disturbed for a while. Read the following prayer:

Lord,
why is this relationship thingy
so tough?
Come on, why couldn't you have sorted this out
before you allowed two people
to become mutually exclusive?
If you're honest,
and isn't that something you're quite big on?
you have to admit
that we're an odd species.
I don't agree that women come from one planet
and men from another.
I think they are from different universes.
Did you have a bit of a giggle
when you took a rib from Adam
and made him a companion?
I think you may have conned him

by saying that it would only cost a rib,
'cos you forgot to say
it would cost him an arm and a leg later
just to keep her happy!
Hey, I'm only joking,
it works both ways.
She likes to be flattered
and given gifts
while he's trying to find the courage
to whisper, lovingly in her ear,
he's supposed to be going down the pub with his mates.
Being honest
is too tough at times.
To admit that you might,
just a fraction, a teeny-weeny bit,
be out of order,
and saying it out loud,
feels like you've just confessed
to being a serial bone-cruncher
(she's a vegetarian you know).
I know, I'm avoiding the issue,
just like I do
when me and my significant other
have a blazing row
about why it's OK
for me to be wrong, and not admit it,
when she is forced to plead guilty
when she hasn't a clue
what I'm on about.
Saying sorry
through gritted teeth
not only sounds strange
but doesn't do your teeth any good either.
I need, no, I think we both need
to ask for your help
whenever we're finding the going tough,
which is pretty much

most of the time.
But all I can ask
is that you'll be with us,
love us, and hug us,
when the last thing we feel like doing is hugging each other.

Violence _____

How we react to situations says a lot about who we are. We all have bad hair days and we all have good gel days! But if you think about it, it's those gut-turning days that stick in the memory.

It says a lot about us that we all too often think of the negative before we consider the positive. In much the same way we are somehow able to remember the dodgy way people behave in full, glorious technicolour. Try it. Just think about some of the people you've met recently and, in particular, those whose behaviour wouldn't look out of place in a riot. See? You can recall almost every detail of their actions. Now, cast your mind back over the last couple of hours. OK? Right, now try and remember all the people you've seen, spoken to or worked with. Can you remember every detail of their actions or conversation?

Whether we like it or not, violent or anti-social behaviour makes an impact . . . ouch!

Taking a step back and gulping air for a few seconds isn't an easy option. Often it takes less time to react to a situation, or circumstance, than it does for the cogs and wheels to turn and put our brain into gear. Have a go at the quiz below and see how you score on the reaction scale.

The Reactor!

1. You've been waiting to use the bathroom for an eternity. Your brother has spent the last hour messing with his hair, washing his feet (three times), cleaning his teeth and filing his nails. As he eventually emerges from the perfumed pit (scent courtesy of Aunt Sally), you walk into the bathroom to find wet towels on the floor, toothpaste all over the sink and he's forgotten to flush the toilet. Do you:

   a. Chase after him, wrap the wet towels around his throat and squeeze toothpaste onto his neatly gelled hair?

   b. Shout the name of every animal that you can remember, and tell him that he reminds you of each of them?

   c. Bite your lip, keep your tongue firmly wedged in your mouth and clean up after him?

2. The packet containing your last chocolate biscuit is sitting on your desk staring at you. You've been saving it for this moment. The moment when you can ignore everyone and everything and indulge in a well-earned cup of tea and *that* biscuit. Just as you're pouring the milk into your cup of tea, a so-called friend of yours walks by and pops your remaining chocolate biscuit into their mouth. Do you:

   a. Offer them your cup of tea and hope it tastes awful?

   b. Suggest that they immediately go and buy you another biscuit?

   c. Smile nicely as you sweep everything off your desk and ask them if there is anything else they'd like to take?

3. You've just taken delivery of a parcel containing a new mobile phone. After reading the instructions, you attempt to use the phone but all it will do is *bleep* annoyingly. Do you:

   a. Read the instructions through again?

   b. Throw the phone at the nearest wall?

   c. Ring the phone company and offer them a few words of advice?

4. You've just finished your late shift at the supermarket. You sit down to relax by watching the film you taped

the previous night. You press play on the remote control, only to find that you'd taped the wrong programme. Do you:

a. Flick through the TV channels in an attempt to find something else to watch?

b. Bury the remote control in the garden?

c. Remove the video cassette from the recorder and stamp on it?

5. You eagerly open the morning mail to see if you've received a reply to your job application. Excitedly, you tear open the envelope and read the enclosed letter of rejection. Do you:

a. Phone the company who sent you the letter, and tell them what they can do with their job?

b. Shrug your shoulders and look at the job vacancies advertised in the local newspaper?

c. Tear the rejection letter up into a hundred small pieces?

6. It's been one of *those* days when if it hasn't gone wrong, it wasn't worth bothering about in the first place. Eager to chat with someone about life, the universe and the shape of bananas, you telephone someone you consider to be a good friend. When they answer the phone, it's obvious they would rather be watching a documentary about bricklaying than talking to you. Do you:

a. Ask them how their day has been?

b. Sigh deeply and tell them you must ring off as you've got something to put in the oven (and under your breath whisper 'your head on a plate')?

c. Tell them that you're sorry, but you must finish your conversation and phone somebody who can understand words of more than two syllables?

7. It's midnight, you have an assignment to hand in the next morning and your computer has decided to go into cyber-sleep. Do you:

   a. Hit the computer with a software manual and tell it to get its act together or else?

   b. Hunt for a pen and paper and drink pots of coffee?

   c. Make a list of twenty excuses to try out on your tutor?

8. You try to phone an order through to your book club. After dialling, the digital switchboard asks you to press the star key twice, gives you a choice of ten options to choose from, and when you press the number you require you are told that all their operators are currently dealing with other customers. Do you:

   a. Put your phone on permanent redial?

   b. Take the time out to relax and listen to the courtesy music?

   c. Send a stream of continuous emails ordering thirty cubic metres of quick-setting concrete?

9. It's Christmas. You've been dropping hints since January to ensure that everybody gets you the presents you want. A pile of discarded wrapping paper later and nobody has got you what you want. Do you:

   a. Take all your presents to your room and throw them under the bed?

   b. Pick each of your presents up in turn and make gagging noises at them?

   c. Thank everybody and think of ways to make your hints less subtle?

10. You buy a car from a friend. You think you've paid a fair price for it until you discover that it needs a lot of money spent on it before you can drive it. Do you:

a. Return the car to your friend and ask for your money back?

b. Cancel the cheque and write a new cheque for the car less the amount it will cost you to get it on the road?

c. Go around to their house and super-glue the locks on their new car?

Find your total score using the following answer guide:

1. a = 0	b = 1	c = 2		6. a = 2	b = 1	c = 0
2. a = 1	b = 2	c = 0		7. a = 0	b = 2	c = 1
3. a = 2	b = 0	c = 1		8. a = 1	b = 2	c = 0
4. a = 2	b = 1	c = 0		9. a = 1	b = 0	c = 2
5. a = 0	b = 2	c = 1		10. a = 2	b = 1	c = 0

Add your total points scored together and discover how you rate in the generosity stakes.

15-20 points
You are one totally cool ice-cube. How do you do it? Perhaps you ought to look through the questions again and put some honest answers in!

Then again, if you arrive at the same score, well, what can you say? You're either a delight to be with or a bit of a goody two-shoes. Possibly you should learn how to express yourself a little more. Sometimes it's good to let people know how you feel. You don't have to go nuclear to get your point across. If you prefer not to get involved in rash displays of emotion, or would rather not confront the issue, then I suggest you take up a contact sport.

6-14 points
Not bad. You seem to have a fair balance of control and self-expression, although at times it would appear that it may only take a slight spark to make you explode. At these times it is necessary to try and take a step back and examine the situation coolly. It might be even more

preferable to turn your back and walk away from the situation altogether.

You might like to consider looking at how you react to different situations and try to find out what makes you explode. Once you've identified these problem areas, try to think of strategies to either avoid these issues or develop ways of dealing with them that leave your head in one piece.

0-5 points
Oooh! I wouldn't want to meet you in a dark alley after a shower of rain. You are a walking volcano, ready to erupt at the slightest tremor. One of the first questions anyone would ask is whether you have any friends.

Seriously, though, think about how you react for a moment. Is it really worth the hassle? All that energy expended in continuous eruptions can't be too good for the heart, can it? Much more of this type of behaviour and you'll be a prime candidate for a heart attack and a lengthy stay in hospital with visitors bringing you bags of fruit (that's if you have anyone left to call a friend).

You have to tell yourself that some things are just not worth getting your shoe-laces untied for. Try putting the following phrase where you'll see it first thing in the morning: 'Some things don't matter very much and most things don't matter at all.' Before you get all agitated and erupt at that statement, let me explain. Make a list of all those people and things that are really important to you. Look at the list again and divide it in half. Identify those people and things that are *really* important to you, those which you wouldn't like to lose at any cost. Those are the people and things which should be precious to you, which you always attempt to protect. Your relationship with God, your partner and family are more important than anything else.

Relax a little, it might give you a whole new outlook on life.

'Ere we go, 'ere we go, 'ere we go

The story of the Good Samaritan is familiar to almost everyone. It has been used as a parable, drama sketch, monologue and as material for zillions of Church talks. The reason for its popularity is simple, it's a really good story. It contains all the essential bits which keep you listening, watching and wanting to know who did it. There's the good guy, bad guys, conflict and a happy ending; all bits we like to see in a good story.

I make no apologies for the following sketch. It's a reworking of the Good Samaritan story and is used to illustrate a moral, a way of behaving that often goes against other people's expectations.

Characters Spud: A fanatical soccer fan. He never misses a game and quite likes a kick-about after the match (preferably with an opposing supporter's head).

Spit: Another soccer fanatic and best mate of Spud. Spit has been known to indulge in the occasional bout of brick-through-window and prefers a knuckle sandwich to a cheese butty any day of the week.

Bert: A senior citizen who goes to a football match whenever he can afford it. He's got a fiery temper and makes good use of his walking-stick if anyone gets in his way.

Prim: He is the soccer club's chaplain. He doesn't like football, doesn't like crowds and hates hotdogs. Likes nothing better than when the final whistle blows and he can hurry home to a cup of hot tea and slice of fruit-cake.

Proper: She's the daughter of the football club's chairman. Doesn't know why anyone wants to watch football but thinks that some of the players have got nice legs. She hates going to a match if the wind is blowing too strongly; it messes with her hair.

Bob: He owns the local newsagent's, which is situated opposite the football ground. He hates home games as a crowd of supporters always come into his shop and leave with more goods than they've paid for.

Scene A darkened alleyway. Spud and Spit have just left the soccer ground and are celebrating their team's victory. Lying on the ground is Bert. He's obviously injured and in need of help.

Props Soccer clothing for Spud and Spit which should include hats, scarves, hooters and a copy of a football programme. Bert is dressed in shabby clothing, an old jacket with patches, trousers with holes in the knees, a cloth cap and walking-stick. Prim should wear a clerical collar (use a piece of plastic cut from a washing-up bottle), a tweed jacket and carry a briefcase. Proper should wear any clothes that are considered fashionable. Her hair must be immaculate and she wears over-the-top make-up. She carries a mobile phone. Bob should wear simple clothing consisting of a jumper and jeans. Scenery should be kept to a minimum. Use a blank wall/screen as a backdrop for the alleyway. Lighting should be dim with spotlights focused on the immediate area around the actors.

(Spud and Spit are walking with their arms around each other's shoulders. They're delighted that their team has won and celebrate by sharing their vocal talents with anyone who'll listen.)

Spud and **Spit**	*(Singing)* 'Ere we go, 'ere we go, 'ere we go.
Spit	What a cracker of a game, eh?
Spud	Too right, mate. Three nil and we didn't break into a sweat. Nice and easy does it.
Spud and **Spit**	*(Singing)* Three nil, three nil, three nil. *(Slowly start to walk from stage left towards stage right)*
Spit	Too early to go home. D'you fancy indulging in a spot of post-match aggravation?
Spud	Lovely jubbly. All we need is a couple of their supporters and we're in business.
	(They both stand still. They still have their arms around each other's shoulders. They take a quick look around)
Spud and **Spit**	*(Singing)* Kick their 'eds in, kick their 'eds in.
Spud	*(Suddenly stops singing and peers into the gloom at the side of the stage)* Hey, 'ang about. What's that on the floor over there. *(He points to a crumpled heap on the floor. Spud walks over to the heap and prods it with his toe)*
Bert	Aaargh.
	(Spud takes a step back in surprise)
Spud	It's alive.
Spit	*(Walking over to Spud)* Are you sure? *(He prods the heap with his foot)*
Bert	Aaargh!

Spit	It might not be alive, but there's plenty of air left in it.
	(Spud prods heap again)
Bert	Aaargh! Gerrof.
Spit	Hey up, *(nudges Spud)* it's got a voice-box.
Spud	*(Raises hands, palms upwards)* The things people dump nowadays!
Bert	*(Struggles to his knees. Uses walking-stick to lean on)* Gerrof, you pair of good-for-nothing 'ooligans.
Spit	What's griping you, grumps?
Bert	*(Shakes a trembling fist at Spit)* If I were a few years younger, I'd give you what for.
Spud and **Spit**	*(Place hands to face)* Oooh, we're so afraid we just might wet ourselves . . . with laughter.
Bert	That's right, make fun of a senior citizen. You're all the same. Picking on the weak and defenceless is about all you can do.
Spud	*(Leans over Bert, who cowers in fright)* Look 'ere you. *(He points to Spit and himself)* We don't pick on no bag of bones, see? But any more of your lip and we'll dump you and your rags in the nearest bin.
Bert	*(Starts to cough. Holds his chest as if in pain)*
Spit	*(Leans towards Bert)* 'Ere, you all right, mate?
Bert	*(Wipes mouth with the back of his hand)* Seen better days, I 'ave.

Spud   *(Points to ground where Bert sits)* What you doin' here, then?

Bert   I was just making my way to the newsagent's to get a paper. *(Coughs again)* All of a sudden a gang of football yobs comes rushing out of the ground and tramples all over me as if I didn't exist.

Spit   What colour scarves did they have on?

Bert   *(Looks at Spit and Spud)* Different from yours.

Spud   Typical of their supporters. A right bunch of compost dwellers. *(He kneels down beside Bert and places a hand under Bert's arm)* 'Ere mate, lets get you up and see what damage is done.

Bert   *(Struggles to his feet supported by Spud and Spit. Coughs a lot)* I'm all right. You can let go of me. *(Begins to wobble as soon as Spud and Spit let go)*

Spit   *(Immediately moves to support Bert)* You don't look all right to me, mate.

Bert   *(Tries to wrestle free of Spit but is held tight)* Gerrof. I don't need your help.

Spud   You need something, grumps.

Spit   *(Looks to his left and sees a vicar walking towards them)* Hey up, mate. Come and give us a hand over here.

Prim   *(Suddenly stops when he hears Spit's voice)* Yes, what is it?

Spud   We've got a damaged bag of bones here that needs some help.

Prim	*(Looks at watch)* I'm terribly sorry, but I'm in an awful rush and mustn't be late.
Spit	Stuff your rush, mate. Come and give us a hand.
Prim	*(Opens briefcase and takes out a copy of Luke's Gospel. He walks over to Bert and offers him the Gospel)* Here you are, my good man. Take this, read it and be of good cheer. *(Prim walks quickly off stage)*
Bert	*(Holds the Gospel in his hand)* This will do right fine, this will.
Spud	What you on about? What good is a scrap of paper?
Bert	It'll burn nicely on me fire, that will. *(He tucks the Gospel inside his coat)*
Spit	*(Tries to straighten Bert's clothes)* You're in a right mess.
Bert	Don't you be so cheeky, you . . . *(Starts to cough violently)*
	(Proper appears stage right. She pretends not to notice Bert)
Spud	Oi! You. Go and get some help.
Proper	*(Looks across at Bert. She raises her head slightly and uses a posh accent)* Are you addressing me?
Spud	*(Copies accent)* Well, I'm certainly not talking to my dog.
Proper	If you're harassing me, I'll call the police. *(She starts to press buttons on her mobile phone)*

Spit	Do something useful with that gadget and call an ambulance.
Proper	*(Stops using the phone)* I am not accustomed to being told what to do.
Spud	Well, it's about time you were.
Proper	How dare you talk to me in that tone of voice.
Spud	*(Nudges Spit)* Hey up, I've got a tone in my voice. Do you think I ought to see a doctor?
Spit	Nah. I've had one for years and it ain't done me no harm.
Spud	*(Nods at Proper)* Use your gadget to call an ambulance and then come and help us with this old bloke.
Proper	*(Wrinkles her nose)* What? You want me to go near that, that, that . . . *(Bert starts to cough. She shakes her head)* It's revolting. *(She hurries away)*
Spit	*(Calls after the departing figure of Proper)* And a merry Christmas to you, too.
Spud	*(To Proper)* Yeah, if I see you again I'll ruffle your hair up! Come on, Spit, we need to do something with grumps. We can't leave him here.
Bert	*(Sniffs loudly)* I'll be all right, I keep telling you. *(Starts to cough again)*
	(Bob appears and walks over to the group)
Bob	Is everything OK?
Spit	No, it ain't OK. This bloke has had a bit of a rough up and he ain't too good.

Bert	I'm all right I tell you.
Bob	*(Peers at Bert)* Bert?
Bert	What?
Bob	I hardly recognised you. Just look at the state you're in.
Spit	It were a group of their supporters that did it.
Spud	They ain't got no respect, that's their problem.
Bob	Come on, we need to get Bert into the warm.
Spit	At last, someone with a bit of common sense.
Spud	Thank goodness for that. *(Turns to Bob)* Look 'ere, mate, *(He hands Bob a few banknotes)* see that he gets what he needs and get him a taxi home.
Bob	*(Takes the money but looks a bit surprised)* Er, are you sure, lads?
Spit	Take it. Just make sure the old bloke gets sorted.
Spud	We'll drop by tomorrow and see how things are, OK?
Bob	Yeah, right, OK. Can you give me a hand to get him into my shop?
Spit	No problem.
	(Spit and Spud place their arms around Bert and help him to walk)
Bert	*(Coughs)* You're OK, you lads are.
Spud	Sssh! Keep a lid on it, grumps. We can't have our reputation damaged.

Spit   Yeah, some things in life are best kept quiet. Know what I mean?

(The four slowly walk off stage. Spud and Spit start to sing 'Ere we go, 'ere we go, 'ere we go)

Reflect

• Does violence ever solve the problem?
• Is violence used as a last resort or knee-jerk reaction?

Consider

• Is it possible to avoid violence?
• Is non-violence a sign of weakness?

A step further

Getting angry is not, in itself, wrong. There are frequent references in the Bible to God getting angry (see Psalm 7:11) and even Jesus losing his cool (see Mark 3:5), and he even got so angry that he trashed the temple in Jerusalem (see Mark 11:15-19).

In the right context, getting angry is sometimes the only way other people will understand just how much something is irritating us. The problem is how we demonstrate that anger and whether we constantly get angry first and think last.

Getting angry for the right reason is the result of thinking through and trying other alternatives first. Sometimes, though, we are confronted with a situation, or circumstance, which demands an instant response. At these times it isn't getting angry that's difficult, it's how we use our anger that may cause the problem.

The word 'righteous' means to act in the right way, to act wisely. If we kick first and ask questions later, then we can only expect others to treat us the same way.

When Jesus was chatting to his disciples, he gave them this piece of advice:

Don't judge others, and God won't judge you. Don't be hard on others, and God won't be hard on you. Forgive others, and God will forgive you. If you give to others, you will be given a full amount in return. It will be packed down, shaken together, and spilling over into your lap. The way you treat others is the way you will be treated. (Luke 6:37-38)

Not an easy piece of advice, and not an easy way to live. We all get it wrong, too often to count, but it takes a real cool dose of guts to admit you were wrong and apologise.

Time out

Have a look at some of the advice given in Proverbs. Take some time to think about them and possibly consider some of the ways you've behaved recently.

Don't be stupid and believe all you hear; be clever and know where you are headed. Only a stupid fool is never cautious – so be extra careful and stay out of trouble. Fools have quick tempers, and no one likes you if you can't be trusted. Stupidity leads to foolishness; be clever and learn. (Proverbs 14:15-18)

And always remember:

If you churn milk you get butter; if you hit your nose, you get blood – and if you stay angry, you get in trouble.
(Proverbs 30:33)

The environment _____

The controversy surrounding Genetically Modified crops has divided politicians, the public and the Church. Some claim that GM research will lead to cheaper and disease-resistant crops that could prove to be the ecological answer for developing countries, while others say it will lead to environmental disaster.

The majority of people might agree that without scientific research and experimentation, we would still be at the mercy of any passing disease that took a fancy to our life-support system. Many of the foods and medicines that we take for granted are a direct result of research that, at the time, would have attracted criticism. If it wasn't for individuals and groups of like-minded people we might still be struggling to design adequate suspension to combat the ruts that make life less than comfortable for people travelling in vehicles with square wheels.

The GM debate has caused a division of opinion between the UK's Ministry of Agriculture, Fisheries and Food (MAFF), politicians, the Church of England, the British Medical Association, Friends of the Earth, various consumer groups and farmers. Are genetically modified organisms an acceptable, scientific way forward or will it turn out to be an agricultural 'Frankenstein', a monster out of control?

All those in favour . . .

It is estimated that approximately 12 million lives are at risk from the possibility of a famine threatening the countries of the Sudan, Ethiopia, Eritrea, Djibouti and Somalia (collectively known as the 'Horn of Africa').

A famine never arrives without warning. Gradually, wells dry up, crops fail and villages' few edible resources are quickly consumed. With nothing left to eat, the families migrate in search of somewhere to either grow food or receive food aid. Already weakened by a lack of food, the young and elderly are the most vulnerable to dehydration, diarrhoea and TB.

The problem, like its solution, is a complicated mix of natural and human intervention. Continued drought, occasional heavy rains leading to flash floods, crop damage from the weather and pests is exacerbated by prolonged disputes and conflict between neighbouring countries. The ability of these countries to prevent food shortages is limited by the fact that almost half of their population exist on less money each day than you would spend on a newspaper and chocolate bar. Even in a relatively normal year, almost 50 per cent of children remain malnourished.

The continual dependency on food aid ensures that each country is vulnerable to the vagaries of the weather and political whim of the donor. Even more disconcerting is the fact that food aid, although necessary, doesn't address the underlying problems of crop failure.

The Biotech companies behind GM research believe that the genetic manipulation of seed can provide the ecological answer to vulnerable countries. By altering the genetic structure of plants they can be made immune to pest attack, disease and drought, and the overall quality of food improved. Rather than being reliant on food aid, the countries most at risk to crop failure will eventually be able to tackle the long-term problems which affect their agriculture.

GM technology also means that foodstuffs will have a longer shelf-life, require far less chemicals to keep them disease resistant, free from pests and increase productivity. This, it is hoped, will reduce costs to the farmer and result in increased profits.

The criticism of GM research centres largely upon the 'unknown' consequences of genetic engineering. Trials of GM crops have become the target of demonstrators and many farmers are reluctant to take part in the trials for fear of vandalism and damage to their other crops.

 If all testing of GM crops were to be stopped it would be difficult to assess the benefits and potential undesirable effects of genetic engineering. The 'unknown' factors, which critics argue pose an ecological threat, would only become 'known' factors as a result of scientific evidence.

Genetic modification of plants and animals is as old as farming itself. The use of selective breeding and cross-fertilisation of plants has been commonplace for centuries. The potential benefits of Genetically Modified Organisms far outweigh any possible disadvantages.

All those against . . .

Plants are usually modified in two distinct ways. The first way is by the careful selection and breeding using cross-fertilisation to achieve the desired results. This method has been in operation for centuries and has led to the range of plants and farm animals that we recognise today. It is a very long process, which requires a certain amount of trial and error and an enormous amount of patience.

The second method is by identifying and retrieving specific genes from one species and inserting it, bio-mechanically or biologically, into the DNA of another species. One example is the idea that a gene from a fish, such as the Arctic Flounder, can be inserted into a strawberry to make it resistant to frost damage. It is this method which is commonly referred to as Genetically Modified Organisms (GMOs).

The supposed links between GMOs and an improved lifestyle are questionable. One of the very real dangers is the potential risk that GMOs pose to health. Although it is acknowledged that there is insufficient research being carried out into GM foods, recent trials of feeding GM potatoes to rats resulted in the development of brain disorders.

The environmental threat of GMOs is a further cause for concern. In Britain, the Department of the Environment has agreed to seventy-three sites for GM trials during 2001. The trials include oilseed-rape, maize and beet crops. Some of the trial sites are being planted with autumn-sown oilseed rape which, many environmentalists believe, will disturb the natural balance of the countryside. Even more disconcerting is the effect of GM crops on wildlife. Evidence shows that some insect and animal life is being threatened as a direct result of exposure to GMOs. Although the GM crops are modified so that they are more resistant to disease and faster growing, the genetic modification has, after the seeds have been eaten, affected the life cycle of wildlife.

The trials also pose a threat to other crops. Many of the GM crops are sterile (the seeds cannot be sown the following year). This has two major setbacks. Firstly, widespread use of GM crops will force farmers to buy new seed each year from the GM companies (resulting in ever-increasing profits for the already large companies). This is one of the main concerns regarding the use of GMOs in developing countries. Those countries, already in serious debt, will become even further indebted to the Western economies as a direct result of being forced to purchase seeds each year from the seed companies. The suggestion that GM crops would solve the food shortages, and make famine a thing of the past, totally ignores the underlying problems of land management, appropriate use of technology and political unrest.

The second concern regards the cross-pollination of the sterile GM crops with organic crops. Although it is suggested that a buffer-zone of up to 200 metres should be established between the GM and non-GM crops, the success of any buffer-zone would be entirely dependent upon the speed and direction of the wind.

GM crops are also said to be a viable way of introducing antibacterial treatments into our diet. The modification of apples and strawberries to protect against tooth decay appears to ignore the fact that one of the main causes of decay is in the consumption of foods that attack the enamel of our teeth. These foods also cause other health problems that cannot be addressed using modified foods.

The development of GM foods appears to deal with the symptoms of intensive agriculture, with its dependency on the increasing use of chemicals, rather than upon the causes of food shortages, health problems and financial dependence. The limited amount of research currently carried out provides insufficient evidence as to the usefulness of GMOs, for in the case of BSE (mad cow disease), symptoms were being recorded a long time before any scientific evidence proved partially conclusive. In other words, why should GM ingredients be introduced into the food chain (ingredients containing less than 2 per cent of GM products are not legally required to be labelled), when there is the suggestion that GMOs may pose a possible health risk?

Reflect

- Do we tend to look at the symptoms of a problem before we examine the cause?
- Who really benefits from scientific advancement?

Consider

- Do you think that we are attempting to 'play God' by trying to alter the genetic make-up of plants and animals?
- Is it right to openly criticise and act against individuals and organisations whose behaviour we disagree with?

A step further

In the beginning, God gave Adam a really responsible job to do, and that was to care for the Garden of Eden and to look after it (see Genesis 2:15). It is generally recognised that this responsibility to care for and look after the land is still valid for humankind.

It would seem that as society has progressed and developed its technological understanding, we've moved further away from an appreciation and understanding of the earth. There appears to be a philosophy of 'we know what we're doing' and a 'we can fix it' mentality, when all along we're not very conscious of the consequences of our actions.

The dependence upon science and technology to solve whatever problem may arise may not only be arrogant but totally naïve. The 'let's see what happens' approach is blundering about in the dark. To risk human life and wreak havoc with nature, without any comprehension of the possible outcome, could be considered an act of outright stupidity. At times, some risks have to be taken, but it really matters what motivates our risk-taking. Is trying to improve the environment and the wellbeing and health of people the primary motivation, or is it greed?

Not only do we have a responsibility to each other, we have a responsibility to God to justify our behaviour. If we kept that thought in our heads as we experiment with nature, I wonder if we'd behave any differently?

Time out

Take some time to read the following extract from the book of Proverbs. This is taken from a section entitled: 'Parental advice on the importance of seeking wisdom and not being foolish'. See what you think.

Wisdom shouts in the streets wherever crowds gather. She shouts in the market places and near the city gates as she says to the people, 'How much longer will you enjoy being stupid fools? Won't you ever stop sneering and laughing at knowledge? Listen as I correct you and tell you what I think. You completely ignored me and refused to listen; you rejected my advice and paid no attention when I warned you. So when you are struck by some terrible disaster, or when trouble and distress surround you like a whirlwind, I will laugh and make fun of you. You will ask for my help, but I won't listen; you will search, but you won't find me. No, you would not learn, and you refused to respect the Lord. You rejected my advice and paid no attention when I warned you. Now you will eat the fruit of what you have done, you are stuffed full with your own schemes. Sin and self-satisfaction bring destruction and death to stupid fools. But if you listen to me, you will be safe and secure without fear of disaster.' (Proverbs 1:20-33)